By Derek Walcott

POEMS

Selected Poems
The Gulf
Another Life
Sea Grapes
The Star-Apple Kingdom
The Fortunate Traveller

PLAYS

Dream on Monkey Mountain and Other Plays
The Joker of Seville and O Babylon!
Remembrance and Pantomime

The Fortunate Traveller

THE FORTUNATE TRAVELLER

Derek Walcott

FARRAR · STRAUS · GIROUX

NEW YORK

Published simultaneously in Canada by McGraw-Hill Ryerson Ltd., Toronto

Printed in the United States of America

Designed by Jeffrey Schaire

First edition, 1981

Acknowledgments are made to KENYON REVIEW, THE NEW YORK REVIEW OF BOOKS, THE AMERICAN POETRY REVIEW, THE TRINIDAD AND TOBAGO REVIEW, COLUMBIA, THE NATION, and LONDON MAGAZINE, where some of these poems originally appeared. "Archipelagoes," "The Cove," "Roman Outposts," "From This Far," "Europa," "Greece," "Cantina Music," and "Easter" (as "The Shadow") were first published by ANTAEUS; "Old New England," "Upstate," "North and South," "Jean Rhys," "The Hotel Normandie Pool," "The Season of Phantasmal Peace," and "Store Bay" originally appeared in THE NEW YORKER

Library of Congress Cataloging in Publication Data

Walcott, Derek.

 The fortunate traveller.

 I. Title.

PR9272.9.W3F6

1981   811   81–9865

  AACR2

For Joseph Brodsky

Contents

[I I I] N O R T H

N O R T H

Upstate

A knife blade of cold air keeps prying
the bus window open. The spring country
won't be shut out. The door to the john
keeps banging. There're a few of us:
a stale-drunk or stoned woman in torn jeans,
a Spanish-American salesman, and, ahead,
a black woman folded in an overcoat.
Emptiness makes a companionable aura
through the upstate villages—repetitive,
but crucial in their little differences
of fields, wide yards with washing, old machinery—where people live
with the highway's patience and flat certainty.

Sometimes I feel sometimes
the Muse is leaving, the Muse is leaving America.
Her tired face is tired of iron fields,
its hollows sing the mines of Appalachia,
she is a chalk-thin miner's wife with knobbled elbows,
her neck tendons taut as banjo strings,
she who was once a freckled palomino with a girl's mane
galloping blue pastures plinkety-plunkety,
staring down at a tree-stunned summer lake,
when all the corny calendars were true.
The departure comes over me in smoke
from the far factories.

But were the willows lyres, the fanned-out pollard willows
with clear translation of water into song,
were the starlings as heartbroken as nightingales,
whose sorrow piles the looming thunderhead
over the Catskills, what would be their theme?
The spring hills are sun-freckled, the chaste white barns flash
through screening trees the vigor of her dream,
like a white plank bridge over a quarreling brook.
Clear images! Direct as your daughters
in the way their clear look returns your stare,
unarguable and fatal—
no, it is more sensual.
I am falling in love with America.

I must put the cold small pebbles from the spring
upon my tongue to learn her language,
to talk like birch or aspen confidently.
I will knock at the widowed door
of one of these villages
where she will admit me like a broad meadow,
like a blue space between mountains,
and holding her arms at the broken elbows
brush the dank hair from a forehead
as warm as bread or as a homecoming.

Old New England

Black clippers, tarred with whales' blood, fold their sails
entering New Bedford, New London, New Haven.
A white church spire whistles into space
like a swordfish, a rocket pierces heaven
as the thawed springs in icy chevrons race
down hillsides and Old Glories flail
the crosses of green farm boys back from 'Nam.
Seasons are measured still by the same
span of the veined leaf and the veined body
whenever the spring wind startles an uproar
of marching oaks with memories of a war
that peeled whole counties from the calendar.

The hillside is still wounded by the spire
of the white meetinghouse, the Indian trail
trickles down it like the brown blood of the whale
in rowanberries bubbling like the spoor
on logs burnt black as Bibles by hellfire.
The war whoop is coiled tight in the white owl,
stone-feathered icon of the Indian soul,
and railway lines are arrowing to the far
mountainwide absence of the Iroquois.
Spring lances wood and wound, and a spring runs
down tilted birch floors with their splintered suns
of beads and mirrors—broken promises
that helped make this Republic what it is.

The crest of our conviction grows as loud
as the spring oaks, rooted and reassured
that God is meek but keeps a whistling sword;
His harpoon is the white lance of the church,
His wandering mind a trail folded in birch,
His rage the vats that boiled the melted beast
when the black clippers brought (knotting each shroud
round the crosstrees) our sons home from the East.

American Muse

No billboard model
but a woman, gaunt,
in a freckled print,
some bony aunt
whose man broke down at the steel mill,
whose daughter chews wild grain in some commune in Arizona,
whose son is a wreath of dried corn
nailed to the door;

Muse of the emigrants,
Walker Evans's Muse,
hugging her ribs,
she wouldn't let you in,
she'd soon be phoning
the State Police;

but she has grown so thin,
so care-concerned,
that wind-burned
hollow face,
the way her mouth winces,
thin as a stick fence,
quiet as cancer.
I pity her. I guess
I would like her well.

Dreamer down afternoon highways—
Trailways fantasist—
through whose transparent profile
the meadows and towns revolve,
who still believes in
the apparition of wingless angels,
like that one who stands on the verge
of the hurtling turnpike
thumbing a ride from the surge
of ignorant traffic.

Piano Practice

[F O R   M A R K   S T R A N D]

April, in another fortnight, metropolitan April.
A drizzle glazes the museum's entrance,
like their eyes when they leave you, equivocating Spring!
The sun dries the avenue's pumice façade
delicately as a girl tamps tissue on her cheek;
the asphalt shines like a silk hat,
the fountains trot like percherons round the Met,
clip, clop, clip, clop in Belle Epoque Manhattan,
as gutters part their lips to the spring rain—
down avenues hazy as Impressionist clichés,
their gargoyle cornices,
their concrete flowers on chipped pediments,
their subway stops in Byzantine mosaic—
the soul sneezes and one tries to compile
the collage of a closing century,
the epistolary pathos, the old Laforguean ache.

Deserted plazas swept by gusts of remorse,
rain-polished cobbles where a curtained carriage
trotted around a corner of Europe for the last time,
as the canals folded like concertinas.
Now fever reddens the trouble spots of the globe,
rain drizzles on the white iron chairs in the gardens.
Today is Thursday, Vallejo is dying,
but come, girl, get your raincoat, let's look for life
in some café behind tear-streaked windows,
perhaps the *fin de siècle* isn't really finished,

maybe there's a piano playing it somewhere,
as the bulbs burn through the heart of the afternoon
in the season of tulips and the pale assassin.
I called the Muse, she pleaded a headache,
but maybe she was just shy at being seen
with someone who has only one climate,
so I passed the flowers in stone, the sylvan pediments,
alone. It wasn't I who shot the archduke,
I excuse myself of all crimes of that ilk,
muttering the subway's obscene graffiti;
I could offer her nothing but the predictable
pale head-scarf of the twilight's lurid silk.

Well, goodbye, then, I'm sorry I've never gone
to the great city that gave Vallejo fever.
Maybe the Seine outshines the East River,
maybe, but near the Metropolitan
a steel tenor pan
dazzlingly practices something from old Vienna,
the scales skittering like minnows across the sea.

North and South

Now, at the rising of Venus—the steady star
that survives translation, if one can call this lamp
the planet that pierces us over indigo islands—
despite the critical sand flies, I accept my function
as a colonial upstart at the end of an empire,
a single, circling, homeless satellite.
I can listen to its guttural death rattle in the shoal
of the legions' withdrawing roar, from the raj,
from the Reich, and see the full moon again
like a white flag rising over Fort Charlotte,
and sunset slowly collapsing like the flag.

It's good that everything's gone, except their language,
which is everything. And it may be a childish revenge
at the presumption of empires to hear the worm
gnawing their solemn columns into coral,
to snorkel over Atlantis, to see, through a mask,
Sidon up to its windows in sand, Tyre, Alexandria,
with their wavering seaweed spires through a glass-bottom boat,
and to buy porous fragments of the Parthenon
from a fisherman in Tobago, but the fear exists,
Delenda est Carthago on the rose horizon,

and the side streets of Manhattan are sown with salt,
as those in the North all wait for that white glare
of the white rose of inferno, all the world's capitals.
Here, in Manhattan, I lead a tight life

and a cold one, my soles stiffen with ice
even through woollen socks; in the fenced back yard,
trees with clenched teeth endure the wind of February,
and I have some friends under its iron ground.
Even when spring comes with its rain of nails,
with its soiled ice oozing into black puddles,
the world will be one season older but no wiser.

Fragments of paper swirl round the bronze general
of Sheridan Square, syllables of Nordic tongues
(as an Obeah priestess sprinkles flour on the doorstep
to ward off evil, so Carthage was sown with salt);
the flakes are falling like a common language
on my nose and lips, and rime forms on the mouth
of a shivering exile from his African province;
a blizzard of moths whirls around the extinguished lamp
of the Union general, sugary insects crunched underfoot.

You move along dark afternoons where death
entered a taxi and sat next to a friend,
or passed another a razor, or whispered "Pardon"
in a check-clothed restaurant behind her cough—
I am thinking of an exile farther than any country.
And, in this heart of darkness, I cannot believe
they are now talking over palings by the doddering
banana fences, or that seas can be warm.

How far I am from those cacophonous seaports
built round the single exclamation of one statue
of Victoria Regina! There vultures shift on the roof
of the red iron market, whose patois
is brittle as slate, a gray stone flecked with quartz.
I prefer the salt freshness of that ignorance,
as language crusts and blackens on the pots
of this cooked culture, coming from a raw one;
and these days in bookstores I stand paralyzed

by the rows of shelves along whose wooden branches
the free-verse nightingales are trilling "Read me! Read me!"
in various metres of asthmatic pain;
or I shiver before the bellowing behemoths
with the snow still falling in white words on Eighth Street,
those burly minds that barrelled through contradictions
like a boar through bracken, or an old tarpon
bristling with broken hooks, or an old stag
spanielled by critics to a crag at twilight,

the exclamation of its antlers like a hat rack
on which they hang their theses. I am tired of words,
and literature is an old couch stuffed with fleas,
of culture stuffed in the taxidermist's hides.
I think of Europe as a gutter of autumn leaves
choked like the thoughts in an old woman's throat.

But she was home to some consul in snow-white ducks
doing out his service in the African provinces,
who wrote letters like this one home and feared malaria
as I mistrust the dark snow, who saw the lances of rain

marching like a Roman legion over the fens.
So, once again, when life has turned into exile,
and nothing consoles, not books, work, music, or a woman,
and I am tired of trampling the brown grass,
whose name I don't know, down an alley of stone,
and I must turn back to the road, its winter traffic,
and others sure in the dark of their direction,
I lie under a blanket on a cold couch,
feeling the flu in my bones like a lantern.

Under the blue sky of winter in Virginia
the brick chimneys flute white smoke through skeletal lindens,
as a spaniel churns up a pyre of blood-rusted leaves;
there is no memorial here to their Treblinka—
as a van delivers from the ovens loaves
as warm as flesh, its brakes jaggedly screech
like the square wheel of a swastika. The mania
of history veils even the clearest air,
the sickly-sweet taste of ash, of something burning.

And when one encounters the slow coil of an accent,
reflexes step aside as if for a snake,

with the paranoid anxiety of the victim.
The ghosts of white-robed horsemen float through the trees,
the galloping hysterical abhorrence of my race—
like any child of the Diaspora, I remember this
even as the flakes whiten Sheridan's shoulders,
and I remember once looking at my aunt's face,
the wintry blue eyes, the rusty hair, and thinking

maybe we are part Jewish, and felt a vein
run through this earth and clench itself like a fist
around an ancient root, and wanted the privilege
to be yet another of the races they fear and hate
instead of one of the haters and the afraid.
Above the spiny woods, dun grass, skeletal trees,
the chimney serenely fluting something from Schubert—
like the wraith of smoke that comes from someone burning—
veins the air with an outcry that I cannot help.

The winter branches are mined with buds,
the fields of March will detonate the crocus,
the olive battalions of the summer woods
will shout orders back to the wind. To the soldier's mind
the season's passage round the pole is martial,
the massacres of autumn sheeted in snow, as
winter turns white as a veterans hospital.
Something quivers in the blood beyond control—
something deeper than our transient fevers.

But in Virginia's woods there is also an old man
dressed like a tramp in an old Union greatcoat,
walking to the music of rustling leaves, and when
I collect my change from a small-town pharmacy,
the cashier's fingertips still wince from my hand
as if it would singe hers—well, yes, *je suis un singe*,
I am one of that tribe of frenetic or melancholy
primates who made your music for many more moons
than all the silver quarters in the till.

SOUTH

A Sea Change

Islands hissing in rain,
light rain and governments falling.
Follow, through cloud, again,
the bittern's lonely calling.

Can this be the right place?
These islands of the blest,
cheap package tours replaced
by politics, rain, unrest?

The edge-erasing mist
through which the sun was splayed
in radials has grayed
the harbor's amethyst,

but a slow, somberer change
than rain keeps blotting out
mountain and mountain range
to an indigo cutout,

as if those scissors could
childishly simplify
geography, or is the Flood
having a second try,

with orders to collect
all the dark-gathering rage
of a bruised electorate
tired of its billboard image

on the hotel-crusted reef
from Pigeon Point to Nassau,
the sand's white, gritted teeth,
its "yes, sir," and "no, sir"?

The rain moves like the law,
slowly; the bays are like
the green fatigues of Cuba—
a monochromatic lake

whose radical romance is
erasing, as it spreads,
all of the sunny answers
with shag-haired thunderheads.

This is no brief unrest
of factions making waves—
the sea is pacifist
deep down; its graves

a wrinkled mirror, hit
by the astonished cries
of bitterns, drag the weight
of chains of centuries.

Beachhead

[FOR TONY HECHT]

I come up to a break
on the beach where a channel
of the river is pushed back
by the ancestral quarrel

of fresh water with salt.
Under it: scalloped sand.
Not caring who's at fault,
I turn and cross inland.

A sepia lagoon
bobbing with coconuts—
helmets from the platoon
of some Marine unit—

whose channel links those years
of boyhood photographs
in *Life* or *Collier's*
to dim Pacific surf.

Sandpipers burst like white
notes from a ceremonial band,
circle, then, on wet sand,
discuss their cancelled flight.

The beach is hot, the fronds
of yellow dwarf palms rust,
the clouds are close as friends,
the sea has not learned rest,

exploding, but not in,
thank heaven, that rhetoric
all wars must be fought in,
I break a brittle stick

pointlessly and walk on,
holding the stick, until
it hefts like a weapon.
There is nothing to kill.

Guadalcanal and Guam—
they must now look like this
abandoned Navy base
camouflaged in gold palm.

Divisions, dates, and armor
marked here are not enough.
The surf, a plasterer,
smooths a fresh cenotaph.

I hurl the stick and brush
right hand against left hand.
Snipers prowl through the bush
of my dry hair. I stand,

not breathing, till they pass,
and the new world feels sure:
sand and sand-whitened grass,
then a jet's signature.

Map of the New World

[I] ARCHIPELAGOES

At the end of this sentence, rain will begin.
At the rain's edge, a sail.

Slowly the sail will lose sight of islands;
into a mist will go the belief in harbors
of an entire race.

The ten-years war is finished.
Helen's hair, a gray cloud.
Troy, a white ashpit
by the drizzling sea.

The drizzle tightens like the strings of a harp.
A man with clouded eyes picks up the rain
and plucks the first line of the *Odyssey*.

[11] THE COVE

Resound it, surge: the legend of Yseult
in languorous detonations of your surf.
I've smuggled in this bleached prow, rustling shoreward
to white sand guarded by fierce manchineel,
a secret
read by the shadow of a frigate hawk.

This inlet's a furnace.
The leaves flash silver signals to the waves.
Far from the curse of government by race,
I turn these leaves—this book's seditious fault—
to feel her skeins of sea mist cross my face,
and catch, on the wind's mouth, a taste of salt.

[III] SEA CRANES

"Only in a world where there are cranes and horses,"
wrote Robert Graves, "can poetry survive."
Or adept goats on crags. Epic
follows the plough, metre the ring of the anvil;
prophecy divines the figurations of storks, and awe
the arc of the stallion's neck.

The flame has left the charred wick of the cypress;
the light will catch these islands in their turn.

Magnificent frigates inaugurate the dusk
that flashes through the whisking tails of horses,
the stony fields they graze.
From the hammered anvil of the promontory
the spray settles in stars.

Generous ocean, turn the wanderer
from his salt sheets, the prodigal
drawn to the deep troughs of the swine-black porpoise.

Wrench his heart's wheel and set his forehead here.

Roman Outposts

[FOR PAT STRACHAN]

The thought-resembling moonlight at a cloud's edge
spreads like the poetry of some Roman outpost
to every corner of the Silver Age.
The moon, capitol of that white empire, is lost
in the black mass. Now, the hot core is Washington,
where once it was Whitehall. Her light burns
all night in office like Cato's ghost,
a concentration ringed with turbulence.
The wet dawn smells of seaweed. On this seawall
where there was a pier once, the concrete cracks
have multiplied like frontiers on a map
of Roman Europe. The same tides rise and fall,
froth, the moon's lantern hung in the same place.
On the sea road skirting the old Navy base,
the archaeologist, with his backpack, crouching
to collect cowries, startles the carbon skeleton
impressed on earth like the gigantic fern
of Caterpillar tracks. By Roman roads
along the sea grapes, their leaves the size
of armor-plates, the stripped hangars rust
where once the bombers left for target practice;
breakers bring rumors of the nuclear fleet
to shells the washed-out blue of pirates' eyes.

From This Far

[FOR ROBERT GIROUX]

[I]

The white almonds of a statue stare
at almond branches wrestling off their shade
like a girl from her dress—a gesture rarely made
by abstract stone.
              A Greek tanker passes
through the net of branches
to the drag of tractors quarrying a cliff—
in its hold, a cargo of marble heads;
from Orpheus to Onassis,
the sea has flown one flag:
white-barred waves on unalterable blue.

The sky's window rattles
at gears raked into reverse;
but no stone head rolls in the ocher dust,
in the soil of our islands no gods are buried.
They were shipped to us, Seferis,
dead on arrival.

[11]

Dawn buckles on the helmet
of rayed Agamemnon.
A net is flung over the shallows;
ocean divides: a bronze door.
In the wash the trunks of warriors
roll and recede.
Great lines, Seferis, have heaved them this far.

At dusk, the man-god bleeds
face down in the veins of the sea.

The blue night hums with bees.
Every hour bores a hole in the hive
of the labyrinth, at whose end
the obscene miscegenation lowers its lyre-curved horns,
and whether it is for dead stones, or the god of thorns,
we stagger the arena with leaking eyes.

The almonds hoard their shadows
as we do the shades of friends.
When a bronze leaf glints, I hear again
the torn throat in the torn shade,
then my eyes harden in a stone head.

I see them in a colonnade
of concrete wharf-piles
where a gull settles.
I hear them groaning with the tractors.
I am eating an ice cream on a hot esplanade,
in a barred blue-and-white vest,
in the brittle shade of a sea grape,
in the iodine reek of shallows,
watching the empty blue port
frothing with yachts,
when a leafy wall
tosses the shadow of a pawing bull.
The Ferryboat passes,
and the gull screeches its message,
opening its wings like a letter,
and the screech grows into a whirlwind
of shawled and ragged crows in a stone field.

[111]

It is during this, Seferis,
that a girl wrestling off her dress
folds with the wave like a dolphin,
that surf hides the sobbing of women,
that, in the thudding of tractors,
I hear the wooden clogs
behind the hills' arena,
and the dry retching of the hunting dogs.

Over something—carrion, the sun's wave-buried king—
vultures with ragged shawls keep circling;
I see the harpist with his eyes like clouds,
I remember you holding a heavy marble head;
I see the other who invited the barbarians
into the whitewashed streets.

I stayed with my own. I starved my hand of names,
no tan fauns leapt over my wrist,
I'll never see Piraeus repeat her white name in water,
but whether my eyes will be white seeds in a bust,
or, likelier, the salt fruit of worms,
they are sockets whose hollows boast
those flashes of inward life,
from the head's thunder-lit storms.

Europa

The full moon is so fierce that I can count the
coconuts' cross-hatched shade on bungalows,
their white walls raging with insomnia.
The stars leak drop by drop on the tin plates
of the sea almonds, and the jeering clouds
are luminously rumpled as the sheets.
The surf, insatiably promiscuous,
groans through the walls; I feel my mind
whiten to moonlight, altering that form
which daylight unambiguously designed,
from a tree to a girl's body bent in foam;
then, treading close, the black hump of a hill,
its nostrils softly snorting, nearing the
naked girl splashing her breasts with silver.
Both would have kept their proper distance still,
if the chaste moon hadn't swiftly drawn the drapes
of a dark cloud, coupling their shapes.

She teases with those flashes, yes, but once
you yield to human horniness, you see
through all that moonshine what they really were,
those gods as seed-bulls, gods as rutting swans—
an overheated farmhand's literature.
Who ever saw her pale arms hook his horns,
her thighs clamped tight in their deep-plunging ride,
watched, in the hiss of the exhausted foam,
her white flesh constellate to phosphorous

as in salt darkness beast and woman come?
Nothing is there, just as it always was,
but the foam's wedge to the horizon-light,
then, wire-thin, the studded armature,
like drops still quivering on his matted hide,
the hooves and horn-points anagrammed in stars.

Greece

Beyond the choric gestures of the olive,
gnarled as sea almonds, over boulders dry
as the calcareous molars of a Cyclops,
past the maniacal frothing of a cave,
I climbed, carrying a body round my shoulders.
I held, for a blade, with armor-dented chops
a saw-toothed agave. Below me, on the sand,
the rooted phalanxes of coconuts,
Trojan and Spartan, stood with rustling helms;
hooking myself up by one bloody hand,
and groaning on each hoist, I made the height
where the sea crows circle, and heaved down the weight
on the stone acre of the promontory.
Up here, at last, was the original story,
nothing was here at all, just stones and light.

I walked to the cliff's edge for a wide look,
relishing this emptiness of sea and air,
the wind filling my mouth said the same word
for "wind," but here it sounded different,
shredding the sea to paper as it rent
sea, wind, and word from their corrupted root;
my memory rode its buffets like a bird.
The body that I had thrown down at my foot
was not really a body but a great book
still fluttering like chitons on a frieze,
till wind worked through the binding of its pages

scattering Hector's and Achilles' rages
to white, diminishing scraps, like gulls that ease
past the gray sphinxes of the crouching islands.

I held air without language in my hands.
My head was scoured of other people's monsters.
I reached this after half a hundred years.
I, too, signed on to follow that gold thread
which linked the spines down a dark library shelf,
around a narrowing catacomb where the dead,
in columns hemmed with gold around the plinth
of their calf-binding, wait, and came upon
my features melting in the Minotaur
at the dead end of the classic labyrinth,
and, with this blade of agave, hacked down
the old Greek bull. Now, crouched before blank stone,
I wrote the sound for "sea," the sign for "sun."

The Man Who Loved Islands

A man is leaning on a cold iron rail
watching an islet from an island and so on,
say, Charlotte Amalie facing St. John,
which begins the concept of infinity
uninterrupted by any mortal sail,
only the thin ghost of a tanker drawing the horizon
behind it with the silvery slick of a snail,
and that's the first shot of this forthcoming film
starring James Coburn and his tanned, leathery, frail
resilience and his now whitening hair,
and his white, vicious grin. Now, we were where?
On this island, one of the Virgins, the prota-
gonist established. Now comes the second shot,
and chaos of artifice still called the plot,
which has to get the hero off somewhere
else, 'cause there's no kick in contemplation
of silvery light upon wind-worried water
between here and the islet of Saint John,
and how they are linked like any silver chain
glinting against the hero's leather chest,
sold in the free gift ports, like noon-bright water.
The hero's momentary rest on the high rail
can be a good beginning. To start with rest
is good—the tanker can come later.
But we can't call it "The Man Who Loved Islands"

any more than some Zen–Karate film
would draw them with "The Hero Who Loves Water."
No soap. There must be something with diamonds,
emeralds, emeralds the color of the shallows there,
or sapphires, like blue, unambiguous air,
sapphires for Sophia, but we'll come to that.
Coburn looks great with or without a hat,
and there must be some minimum of slaughter
that brings in rubies, but you cannot hover
over that first shot like a painting. Action
is all of art, the thoughtless pace
of lying with style, so that when it's over,
that first great shot of Coburn's leathery face,
crinkled like the water which he contemplates,
could be superfluous, in the first place,
since that tired artifice called history,
which in its motion is as false as fiction,
requires an outline, a summary. I can think of none,
quite honestly. I'm no photographer; this
could be a movie. I mean things are moving,
the water for example, the light on the man's hair
that has gone white, even those crescent sands
are just as moving as his love of islands;
the tanker that seems still is moving, even
the clouds like galleons anchored in heaven,
and what is moving most of all of course
is the violent man lulled into this inaction

by the wide sea. Let's hold it on the sea
as we establish their ancient interaction,
a hint of the Homeric, a little poetry
before the whole mess hits the bloody fan.
All these islands that you love, I guaran-
tee we'll work them in as background, with
generous establishing shots from Jim's car and
even a few harbors and villages, *if*
we blow the tanker up and get the flames
blazing with oil, and Sophia, if she's free,
daintily smudged, with her slip daintily torn,
is climbing down this rope ladder, and we shoot up
from Coburn's P.O.V.—he's got the gems—
that's where we throw in Charlotte Amalie
and the waterfront bars, and this Danish alley
with the heavies chasing, and we can keep all the
business of Jim on the rail; that lyric stuff
goes with the credits if you insist on keeping it tend-
er; I can see it, but things must get rough
pretty damn fast, or else you lose them, pally,
or, tell you what, let's save it for THE END.

Hurucan

[I]

Once branching light startles the hair of the coconuts,
and on the villas' asphalt roofs, rain
resonates like pebbles in a pan,
and only the skirts of surf
waltz round the abandoned bandstand,
and we hear the telephone cables
hallooing like fingers tapped over an Indian's mouth,
once the zinc roofs begin wrenching their nails
like freight uncrated with a crowbar,
we remember you as the possible
deity of the whistling marsh-canes,
we doubt that you were ever slain
by the steel Castilian lances
of a thousand horizons,
deity of the yellow-skinned ones
who thatched your temple with plantains.

When the power station's blackout
grows frightening as amnesia,
and the luxury resorts
revert to the spear-tips of candles,
and the swimming pools in their marsh-light
multiply with hysterical lilies
like the beaks of fledglings uttering your name,
when lightning fizzles out

in the wireless, we can see and hear
the streaming black locks of clouds,
flesh the gamboge of lightning,
and the epicanthic, almond-shaped eye
of the whirling cyclops,
runner through the cloud-smoke,
our ocean's marathon strider,
the only survivor
of their massacred deities

whose temples change
like the clouds over Yucatán,
in the copper twilight over Ecuador,
runner who can grip the mares' tails
of galloping cirrus,
vaulting the dead conquistadors of the helmeted palms.
You'd never reply
to the name of the northern messenger
whose zigzagging trident
pitchforks the oaks like straw,
nor to the thunderous tambors
of Shango; you rage
till we get your name right,
till the surf and the bent palms dance
to your tune, even if, at your entrance,
clouds plod the horizon like caparisoned camels,
and the wind begins to unwhirl

like a burnoose; you abhor
all other parallels
but our own,
Hurucan.
You scream like a man whose wife is dead,
like a god who has lost his race,
you yank the electric wires with wet hands.

Then we think of a different name
than the cute ones christened by radar,
in the sludge that sways
next day by the greased pierheads
where a rowboat still rocks in fear,
and Florida now flares to your flashbulb
and the map of Texas rattles,
and we lie awake in the dark
by the dripping stelae of candles,
our heads gigantified on the walls,
and think of you, still running
with tendons feathered with lightning,
water-worrier, whom the chained trees
strain to follow,
havoc, reminder, ancestor,
and, when morning enters, pale
as an insurance broker,
god.

The sea almond's dress
is drenched in the morning,
the leaves drip on their clotheslines
like wax drops from candles,
the pent waves circle their fences
like witless sheep.
A freighter is parked
on the coastal road to the airport,
and the birds won't be back
for some time. The chairs
around the bandstand are heaped up
like the morning after your dance,
and the worms we have buried underground
spark and stutter again. Roofs
are scattered all over the hillsides
like cards dropped during a shoot-out,
and the sea starts the pompous thunder
of a military funeral
as spray shoots up round the kiosk
where the Police Band played.

We return the pieces of fear
to their proper place,
the shelf at the back of the mind—
the artifacts, the Carib arrowheads,

the pin-pierced amulets,
and that force whose weather vanes
are the slow-spinning frigates.
Your name fades again in the grounded
flights; there in dark hangars
the mineral patience of cattle—
a cold sweat slides down the silver
hides of the empty planes.

Jean Rhys

In their faint photographs
mottled with chemicals,
like the left hand of some spinster aunt,
they have drifted to the edge
of verandas in Whistlerian
white, their jungle turned tea-brown—
even its spiked palms—
their features pale,
to be pencilled in:
bone-collared gentlemen
with spiked mustaches
and their wives embayed in the wickerwork
armchairs, all looking colored
from the distance of a century
beginning to groan sideways from the ax stroke!

Their bay horses blacken
like spaniels, the front lawn a beige
carpet, brown moonlight and a moon
so sallow, so pharmaceutical
that her face is a feverish child's,
some malarial angel
whose grave still cowers
under a fury of bush,
a mania of wild yams
wrangling to hide her from ancestral churchyards.

And the sigh of that child
is white as an orchid
on a crusted log
in the bush of Dominica,
a V of Chinese white
meant for the beat of a seagull
over a sepia souvenir of Cornwall,
as the white hush between two sentences.

Sundays! Their furnace
of boredom after church.
A maiden aunt canoes through lilies of clouds
in a Carib hammock, to a hymn's metronome,
and the child on the varnished, lion-footed couch
sees the hills dip and straighten with each lurch.
The green-leaved uproar of the century
turns dim as the Atlantic, a rumorous haze
behind the lime trees, breakers
advancing in decorous, pleated lace;
the cement grindstone of the afternoon
turns slowly, sharpening her senses,
the bay below is green as calalu, stewing Sargasso.

In that fierce hush
between Dominican mountains
the child expects a sound

from a butterfly clipping itself to a bush
like a gold earring to a black maid's ear—
one who goes down to the village, visiting,
whose pink dress wilts like a flower between the limes.

There are logs
wrinkled like the hand of an old woman
who wrote with a fine courtesy to that world
when grace was common as malaria,
when the gas lanterns' hiss on the veranda
drew the aunts out like moths
doomed to be pressed in a book, to fall
into the brown oblivion of an album,
embroiderers of silence
for whom the arches of the Thames,
Parliament's needles,
and the petit-point reflections of London Bridge
fade on the hammock cushions from the sun,
where one night
a child stares at the windless candle flame
from the corner of a lion-footed couch
at the erect white light,
her right hand married to *Jane Eyre*,
foreseeing that her own white wedding dress
will be white paper.

Cantina Music

A lilac sea between shacks,
at the Carenage overpass, the go-light
the exact hue of a firefly's fake emerald.
Coconuts, ringed with blight,
rust onto crusted roofs,
the pirogues soldered
to metal water—then,
firing the mountain range
rose, yellow, orange,
light perforates the black hills like bullet holes.

Hot, hot as ingots,
music glows from the bars.
They lean back like bandidos
in the cantinas circling St. James;
their fantasies
shine like the rain's guitars;
of generals whose names
darken their iron stallions,
against whose dusky faces the palms droop,
morose mustaches of dead liberators.

Bandidos of no republic,
Sonora, Veracruz,
your teeth flashed like daggers,
your snarl was torn leather,
you strode into the street

at the hour of the firefly
and, boots astride for the showdown,
prepared to die
if someone could name the cause,
to play your last scene as
you slowly waltzed into dirt
to a joropo from the tin cantinas.

Widmarks, Zapatas, Djangos,
black hats of the double feature,
your hearts kept losing time
to the ruby thud of the jukebox's
"*adios, muchachos,*
compañeros de mi vida,"
that you play at the grave of some boy shot by the police,
some wrong-sided leader,
tenor-pan man from "Renegades," or
"Gay Desperadoes,"
who fell there
exactly as he had learned to from the screen—
limp as an ocelot
in whose amber eyes
there is no flickering question
of justice.

And the shot that flings
the bandit whirling

in perverse crucifixions
so that each frame, arrested,
repeats itself like a corrupt Pietà,
the prodigal with the Mother of the World,
echoes as deep as any silver mine—
from the rumshops,
from cantinas,
from the sky with a hibiscus in her hair,
from Rio,
from Buenos Aires,
from Carenage,
from St. James—
and has more than they think to do with
the lilac sea between the shacks,
the highway's overpass and the fake emerald
of the go-light
that unexpectedly
remains on red.

The Liberator

In a blue bar at the crossroads, before you turn
into Valencia or Grande, Castilian bequests,
in back of that bar, cool and dark as prison,
where a sunbeam dances through brown rum-bottles
like a firefly through a thicket of cocoa,
like an army torch looking for a guerrilla,
the guerrilla with the gouged Spanish face named
Sonora again climbs the track through wild bananas,
sweat glued to his face like a hot cloth
under the barber's hand. The jungle is steam.
He would like to plunge his hands in those clouds
on the next range. From Grande to Valencia
the blue-green plain below breaks through the leaves.
"Adios, then," said Estenzia. He went downhill.
And the army find him. The world keep the same.
The others get tired of just eating mango,
and fig, carefully fried. They dream of beds.
They bawl for their mudder and their children haunt them.
They dream of mattresses, even those in prison.
For half an hour I, Sonora, sit in the sun
till my face turn copper. And for that half hour,
the spikes of wild palm was Pizarro helmet,
and for that half hour, señor, I ain't look at them.

A fly, big like a bee, dance on my rifle barrel
like he know who was holding it already dead.
I turn: Manuel. Frederico. Marcos. The people

of Hernando Cortes, of Pizarro, El Cid—
men who had flung the pennoned spear flying
to the oaken door, the heart of authority.
We was going so good. But then, they get tired.
For a straight double-rum at a wet zinc table
in a blue bar at the crossroads, before you turn
into Valencia or Grande, Castilian bequests,
Sonora, the socialist, on any given Sunday
will narrate this adventure, which, inevitably,
a loss of heredity needs to create.

The Spoiler's Return

[F O R   E A R L   L O V E L A C E]

I sit high on this bridge in Laventille,
watching that city where I left no will
but my own conscience and rum-eaten wit,
and limers passing see me where I sit,
ghost in brown gabardine, bones in a sack,
and bawl: "Ay, Spoiler, boy! When you come back?"
And those who bold don't feel they out of place
to peel my limeskin back, and see a face
with eyes as cold as a dead macajuel,
and if they still can talk, I answer: "Hell."
I have a room there where I keep a crown,
and Satan send me to check out this town.
Down there, that Hot Boy have a stereo
where, whole day, he does blast my caiso;
I beg him two weeks' leave and he send me
back up, not as no bedbug or no flea,
but in this limeskin hat and floccy suit,
to sing what I did always sing: the truth.
Tell Desperadoes when you reach the hill,
I decompose, but I composing still:

I going to bite them young ladies, partner,
like a hogdog or a hamburger
and if you thin, don't be in a fright
is only big fat women I going to bite.

The shark, racing the shadow of the shark
across clear coral rocks, does make them dark—
that is my premonition of the scene
of what passing over this Caribbean.
Is crab climbing crab-back, in a crab-quarrel,
and going round and round in the same barrel,
is sharks with shirt-jacs, sharks with well-pressed fins,
ripping we small fry off with razor grins;
nothing ain't change but color and attire,
so back me up, Old Brigade of Satire,
back me up, Martial, Juvenal, and Pope
(to hang theirself I giving plenty rope),
join Spoiler' chorus, sing the song with me,
Lord Rochester, who praised the nimble flea:

Were I, who to my cost already am
One of those strange, prodigious creatures, Man,
A spirit free, to choose for my own share,
What case of flesh and blood I pleased to wear,
I hope when I die, after burial,
To come back as an insect or animal.

I see these islands and I feel to bawl,
"area of darkness" with V. S. Nightfall.

Lock off your tears, you casting pearls of grief
on a duck's back, a waxen dasheen leaf,

the slime crab's carapace is waterproof
and those with hearing aids turn off the truth,
and their dark glasses let you criticize
your own presumptuous image in their eyes.
Behind dark glasses is just hollow skull,
and black still poor, though black is beautiful.
So, crown and mitre me Bedbug the First—
the gift of mockery with which I'm cursed
is just a insect biting Fame behind,
a vermin swimming in a glass of wine,
that, dipped out with a finger, bound to bite
its saving host, ungrateful parasite,
whose sting, between the cleft arse and its seat,
reminds Authority man is just meat,
a moralist as mordant as the louse
that the good husband brings from the whorehouse,
the flea whose itch to make all Power wince,
will crash a fete, even at his life's expense,
and these pile up in lime pits by the heap,
daily, that our deliverers may sleep.
All those who promise free and just debate,
then blow up radicals to save the state,
who allow, in democracy's defense,
a parliament of spiked heads on a fence,
all you go bawl out, "Spoils, things ain't so bad."
This ain't the Dark Age, is just Trinidad,
is human nature, Spoiler, after all,

it ain't big genocide, is just bohbohl;
safe and conservative, 'fraid to take side,
they say that Rodney commit suicide,
is the same voices that, in the slave ship,
smile at their brothers, "Boy, is just the whip,"
I free and easy, you see me have chain?
A little censorship can't cause no pain,
a little graft can't rot the human mind,
what sweet in goat-mouth sour in his behind.
So I sing with Attila, I sing with Commander,
what right in Guyana, right in Uganda.
The time could come, it can't be very long,
when they will jail calypso for picong,
for first comes television, then the press,
all in the name of Civic Righteousness;
it has been done before, all Power has
made the sky shit and maggots of the stars,
over these Romans lying on their backs,
the hookers swaying their enormous sacks,
until all language stinks, and the truth lies,
a mass for maggots and a fete for flies;
and, for a spineless thing, rumor can twist
into a style the local journalist—
as bland as a green coconut, his manner
routinely tart, his sources the Savannah
and all pretensions to a native art
reduced to giggles at the coconut cart,

where heads with reputations, in one slice,
are brought to earth, when they ain't eating nice;
and as for local Art, so it does go,
the audience have more talent than the show.

Is Carnival, straight Carnival that's all,
the beat is base, the melody bohbohl,
all Port of Spain is a twelve-thirty show,
some playing Kojak, some Fidel Castro,
some Rastamen, but, with or without locks,
to Spoiler is the same old khaki socks,
all Frederick Street stinking like a closed drain,
Hell is a city much like Port of Spain,
what the rain rots, the sun ripens some more,
all in due process and within the law,
as, like a sailor on a spending spree,
we blow our oil-bloated economy
on projects from here to eternity,
and Lord, the sunlit streets break Spoiler's heart,
to have natural gas and not to give a fart,
to see them line up, pitch-oil tin in hand:
each independent, oil-forsaken island,
like jeering at some scrunter with the blues,
while you lend him some need-a-half-sole shoes,
some begging bold as brass, some coming meeker,
but from Jamaica to poor Dominica
we make them know they begging, every loan

we send them is like blood squeezed out of stone,
and giving gives us back the right to laugh
that we couldn't see we own black people starve,
and, more we give, more we congratulate
we-self on our own self-sufficient state.
In all them project, all them Five-Year Plan,
what happen to the Brotherhood of Man?
Around the time I dead it wasn't so,
we sang the Commonwealth of caiso,
we was in chains, but chains made us unite,
now who have, good for them, and who blight, blight;
my bread is bitterness, my wine is gall,
my chorus is the same: "I want to fall."
Oh, wheel of industry, check out your cogs!
Between the knee-high trash and khaki dogs
Arnold's Phoenician trader reach this far,
selling you half-dead batteries for your car;
the children of Tagore, in funeral shroud,
curry favor and chicken from the crowd;
as for the Creoles, check their house, and look,
you bust your brain before you find a book,
when Spoiler see all this, ain't he must bawl,
"area of darkness," with V. S. Nightfall?
Corbeaux like cardinals line the La Basse
in ecumenical patience while you pass
the Beetham Highway—Guard corruption's stench,
you bald, black justices of the High Bench—

and beyond them the firelit mangrove swamps,
ibises practicing for postage stamps,
Lord, let me take a taxi South again
and hear, drumming across Caroni Plain,
the tabla in the Indian half hour
when twilight fills the mud huts of the poor,
to hear the tattered flags of drying corn
rattle a sky from which all the gods gone,
their bleached flags of distress waving to me
from shacks, adrift like rafts on a green sea,
"Things ain't go change, they ain't go change at all,"
to my old chorus: "Lord, I want to bawl."
The poor still poor, whatever arse they catch.
Look south from Laventille, and you can watch
the torn brown patches of the Central Plain
slowly restitched by needles of the rain,
and the frayed earth, crisscrossed like old bagasse,
spring to a cushiony quilt of emerald grass,
and who does sew and sow and patch the land?
The Indian. And whose villages turn sand?
The fishermen doomed to stitching the huge net
of the torn foam from Point to La Fillette.

One thing with Hell, at least it organize
in soaring circles, when any man dies
he must pass through them first, that is the style,
Jesus was down here for a little while,

cadaverous Dante, big-guts Rabelais,
all of them wave to Spoiler on their way.
Catch us in Satan tent, next carnival:
Lord Rochester, Quevedo, Juvenal,
Maestro, Martial, Pope, Dryden, Swift, Lord Byron,
the lords of irony, the Duke of Iron,
hotly contending for the monarchy
in couplets or the old re-minor key,
all those who gave earth's pompous carnival
fatigue, and groaned "O God, I feel to fall!"
all those whose anger for the poor on earth
made them weep with a laughter beyond mirth,
names wide as oceans when compared with mine
salted my songs, and gave me their high sign.
All you excuse me, Spoiler was in town;
you pass him straight, so now he gone back down.

Port of Spain

Midsummer stretches before me with a cat's yawn.
Trees with dust on their lips, cars melting down
in a furnace. Heat staggers the drifting mongrels.
The capitol has been repainted rose, the rails
round the parks the color of rusting blood;
junta and *coup d'état*, the newest Latino mood,
broods on the balcony. Monotonous lurid bushes
brush the damp air with the ideograms of buzzards
over the Chinese groceries. The oven alleys stifle
where mournful tailors peer over old machines
stitching June and July together seamlessly,
and one waits for lightning as the armed sentry
hopes in boredom for the crack of a rifle—
but I feed on its dust, its ordinariness,
on the inertia that fills its exiles with horror,
on the dust over the hills with their orange lights,
even on the pilot light in the reeking harbor
that turns like a police car's. The terror
is local, at least. Like the magnolia's whorish whiff.
And the dog barks of the revolution crying wolf.

The moon shines like a lost button;
the black water stinks under the sodium lights on
the wharf. The night is turned on as firmly
as a switch, dishes clatter behind bright windows,
I walk along the walls with occasional shadows
that say nothing. Sometimes, in narrow doors

there are old men playing the same quiet games—
cards, draughts, dominoes. I give them names.
The night is companionable, the day is as fierce as
our human future anywhere. I can understand
Borges's blind love of Buenos Aires,
how a man feels the veins of a city swell in his hand.

The Hotel Normandie Pool

[I]

Around the cold pool in the metal light
of New Year's morning, I choose one of nine
cast-iron umbrellas set in iron tables
for work and coffee. The first cigarette
triggers the usual fusillade of coughs.
After a breeze the pool settles the weight
of its reflections on one line. Sunshine
lattices a blank wall with the shade of gables,
stirs the splayed shadows of the hills like moths.

Last night, framed in the binding of that window,
like the great chapter in some Russian novel
in which, during the war, the prince comes home
to watch the soundless waltzers dart and swivel,
like fishes in their lamplit aquarium,
I stood in my own gauze of swirling snow
and, through the parted hair of ribboned drapes,
felt, between gusts of music, the pool widen
between myself and those light-scissored shapes.

The dancers stiffened and, like fish, were frozen
in panes of ice blocked by the window frames;
one woman fanned, still fluttering on a pin,
as a dark fusillade of kettledrums
and a piercing cornet played "Auld Lang Syne"

while a battalion of drunk married men
reswore their vows. For this my fiftieth year,
I muttered to the ribbon-medalled water,
"Change me, my sign, to someone I can bear."

Now my pen's shadow, angled at the wrist
with the chrome stanchions at the pool's edge,
dims on its lines like birches in a mist
as a cloud fills my hand. A drop punctuates
the startled paper. The pool's iron umbrellas
ring with the drizzle. Sun hits the water.
The pool is blinding zinc. I shut my eyes,
and as I raise their lids I see each daughter
ride on the rayed shells of both irises.

The prayer is brief: That the transparent wrist
would not cloud surfaces with my own shadow,
and that this page's surface would unmist
after my breath as pools and mirrors do.
But all reflection gets no easier,
although the brown, dry needles of that palm
quiver to stasis and things resume their rhyme
in water, like the rubber ring that is a
red rubber ring inverted at the line's center.

Into that ring my younger daughter dived
yesterday, slithering like a young dolphin,

her rippling shadow hungering under her,
with nothing there to show how well she moved
but in my mind the veer of limb and fin.
Transparent absences! Love makes me look
through a clear ceiling into rooms of sand;
I ask the element that is my sign,
"Oh, let her lithe head through that surface break!"

Aquarian, I was married to water;
under that certain roof, I would lie still
next to my sister spirit, horizontal
below what stars derailed our parallel
from our far vow's undeviating course;
the next line rises as they enter it,
Peter, Anna, Elizabeth—Margaret
still sleeping with one arm around each daughter,
in the true shape of love, beyond divorce.

Time cuts down on the length man can endure
his own reflection. Entering a glass
I surface quickly now, prefer to breathe
the fetid and familiar atmosphere
of work and cigarettes. Only tyrants believe
their mirrors, or Narcissi, brooding on boards,
before they plunge into their images;
at fifty I have learnt that beyond words
is the disfiguring exile of divorce.

[1 1]

Across blue seamless silk, iron umbrellas
and a brown palm burn. A sandalled man comes out
and, in a robe of foam-frayed terry cloth,
with Roman graveness buries his room key,
then, mummy-oiling both forearms and face
with sunglasses still on, stands, fixing me,
and nods. Some petty businessman who tans
his pallor a negotiable bronze,
and the bright nod would have been commonplace

as he uncurled his shades above the pool's
reflecting rim—white towel, toga-slung,
foam hair repeated by the robe's frayed hem—
but, in the lines of his sun-dazzled squint,
a phrase was forming in that distant tongue
of which the mind keeps just a mineral glint,
the lovely Latin lost to all our schools:
"*Quis te misit, Magister?*" And its whisper went
through my cold body, veining it in stone.

On marble, concrete, or obsidian,
your visit, Master, magnifies the lines
of our small pool to that Ovidian
thunder of surf between the Baltic pines.
The light that swept Rome's squares and palaces,

washing her tangled fountains of green bronze
when you were one drop in a surf of faces—
a fleck of spittle from the she-wolf's tooth—
now splashes a palm's shadow at your foot.

Turn to us, Ovid. Our emerald sands
are stained with sewage from each tin-shacked Rome;
corruption, censorship, and arrogance
make exile seem a happier thought than home.
"Ah, for the calm proconsul with a voice
as just and level as this Roman pool,"
our house slaves sigh; the field slaves scream revenge;
one moves between the flatterer and the fool
yearning for the old bondage from both ends.

And I, whose ancestors were slave and Roman,
have seen both sides of the imperial foam,
heard palm and pine tree alternate applause
as the white breakers rose in galleries
to settle, whispering at the tilted palm
of the boy-god, Augustus. My own face
held negro Neros, chalk Caligulas;
my own reflection slid along the glass
of faces foaming past triumphal cars.

Master, each idea has become suspicious
of its shadow. A lifelong friend whispers

in his own house as if it might arrest him;
markets no more applaud, as was their custom,
our camouflaged, booted militias
roaring past on camions, the sugar-apples
of grenades growing on their belts; ideas
with guns divide the islands; in dark squares
the poems gather like conspirators.

Then Ovid said, "When I was first exiled,
I missed my language as your tongue needs salt,
in every watery shape I saw my child,
no bench would tell my shadow 'Here's your place';
bridges, canals, willow-fanned waterways
turned from my parting gaze like an insult,
till, on a tablet smooth as the pool's skin,
I made reflections that, in many ways,
were even stronger than their origin.

"Tiled villas anchored in their foaming orchards,
parched terraces in a dust cloud of words,
among clod-fires, wolfskins, starving herds,
Tibullus' flute faded, sweetest of shepherds.
Through shaggy pines the beaks of needling birds
pricked me at Tomis to learn their tribal tongue,
so, since desire is stronger than its disease,
my pen's beak parted till we chirped one song
in the unequal shade of equal trees.

"Campaigns enlarged our frontiers like clouds,
but my own government was the bare boards
of a plank table swept by resinous pines
whose boughs kept skittering from Caesar's eye
with every yaw. There, hammering out lines
in that green forge to fit me for the horse,
I bent on a solitude so tyrannous
against the once seductive surf of crowds
that no wife softens it, or Caesar's envy.

"And where are those detractors now who said
that in and out of the imperial shade
I scuttled, showing to a frowning sun
the fickle dyes of the chameleon?
Romans"—he smiled—"will mock your slavish rhyme,
the slaves your love of Roman structures, when,
from Metamorphoses to Tristia,
art obeys its own order. Now it's time."
Tying his toga gently, he went in.

There, at the year's horizon, he had stood,
as if the pool's meridian were the line
that doubled the burden of his solitude
in either world; and, as one leaf fell,
his echo rippled: "Why here, of all places,
a small, suburban tropical hotel,
its pool pitched to a Mediterranean blue,
its palms rusting in their concrete oasis?
Because to make my image flatters you."

[I I I]

At dusk, the sky is loaded like watercolor paper
with an orange wash in which every edge frays—
a painting with no memory of the painter—
and what this pool recites is not a phrase
from an invisible, exiled laureate,
where there's no laurel, but the scant applause
of one dry, scraping palm tree as blue eve-
ning ignites its blossoms from one mango flower,
and something, not a leaf, falls like a leaf,

as swifts with needle-beaks dart, panicking over
the pool's cloud-closing light. For an envoi,
write what the wrinkled god repeats to the boy-
god: "May the last light of heaven pity us
for the hardening lie in the face that we did not tell."
Dusk. The trees blacken like the pool's umbrellas.
Dusk. Suspension of every image and its voice.
The mangoes pitch from their green dark like meteors.
The fruit bat swings on its branch, a tongueless bell.

Early Pompeian

[F O R N O R L I N E]

Ere Babylon was dust,
The Magus Zoroaster, my dead child,
Met his own image walking in the garden,
That apparition, sole of men, he saw.
S H E L L E Y

[I]

In the first years, when your hair
was parted severely in the Pompeian style,
you resembled those mosaics
whose round eyes
keep their immortal pinpoints, or were,
in laughing days, black olives on a saucer.

Then, one night, years later,
a flaring torch passed slowly down that wall
and lit them, and it was your turn.
Your girlhood was finished, your sorrows were robing
you with the readiness of woman.

The darkness placed a black shawl around your shoulders,
pointed to a colonnade of torches
like palm trees with their fronds on fire,
pointed out the cold flagstones to the sacrificial basin

where the priest stands with his birth-sword.
You nodded. You began to walk.

Voices stretched out their hands and you stepped from the wall.

Past the lowering eyes of rumors,
past the unblinking stares of the envious,
as, step by step, it faded
behind you, that portrait
with its plum-parted lips,
the skin of pomegranate,
the forehead's blank, unborn bewilderment.
Now you walked in those heel-hollowed steps
in which all of our mothers before us went.

And they led you, pale as the day-delivered moon,
through the fallen white columns of a hospital
to the volcanic bedrock of mud and screams and fire,

into the lava of the damned birth-blood,
the sacrificial gutters,
to where the eye of the stillborn star showed at the end of your road,
a dying star fighting the viruses
of furious constellations,
through the tangled veins, the vineyard of woman's labor,
to a black ditch under the corpuscles of stars,
where the shrunken grape would be born that would not call you mother.

In your noble, flickering gaze there was that which repeated
to the stone you carried
"The hardest times are the noblest, my dead child,"
and the torch passed its flame to your tongue,
your face bronzed in the drenches and fires of your finest sweat.

In their black sockets, the pebbles of your eyes
rattled like dice in the tin cup of the blind Fates.
On the black wings of your screams I watched vultures rise,
the laser-lances of pain splinter on the gods' breastplates.
Your nerve ends screamed like fifes,
your temples repeated a drum,
and your firelit head, in profile, passed other faces
as a funeral ship passes the torch-lit headlands
with its princely freight,
your black hair billowing like dishevelled smoke.

Your eyelids whitened like knuckles gripping
the incomprehensible, vague sills of pain.
The door creaked, groaning open, and in its draft, no, a whirlwind,
the lamp that was struggling with darkness was blown out
by the foul breeze off the amniotic sea.

[11]

By the black harbor,
the black schooners are tired
of going anywhere; the sea
is black and salt as the mind of a woman after labor.

Child, wherever you are,
I am still your father;
let your small, dead star
rock in my heart's black salt,
this sacrificial basin where I weep;
you passed from a sleep to a sleep
with no pilot, without a light.

Beautiful, black, and salt-warm is the starry night,
the smell off the sea is your mother,
as is this wind that moves in the leaves of the wharf under the
        pavement light.

I stare into black water by whose hulls
heaven is rocked like a cradle,
except, except for one extinguished star,
and I think of a hand that stretches out from her bedside for nothing,
and then is withdrawn, remembering where you are.

[1 1 1]

I will let the nights pass,
I shall allow the sun to rise,
I shall let it pass like a torch along a wall
on which there is fadingly set,
stone by fading stone,
the face of an astonished girl, her lips, her black hair parted
in the early Pompeian style.

And what can I write for her
but that when we are stoned with pain,
and we shake our heads wildly from side to side,
saying "no more," "no more again," to certain things,
no more faith, no more hope, only charity,
charity gives faith and hope much stronger wings.

[I V]

As for you, little star,
my lost daughter, you are
bent in the shape forever
of a curled seed sailing the earth,
in the shape of one question, a comma
that knows before us whether death
is another birth.
            I had no answer
to that tap-tapping under the dome
of the stomach's round coffin.
I could not guess whether you were calling
to be let in, or to be let go
when the door's groaning blaze
seared the grape-skin
frailty of your eyes crying
against our light, and all that is kin
to the light.
You had sailed without any light
your seven months on the amniotic sea.
You never saw your murderer,
your birth and death giver,
but I will see you everywhere,
I will see you in a boneless
sunbeam that strokes the texture
of things—my arm, the pulseless arm

of an armchair, an iron railing, the leaves
of a dusty plant by a closed door,
in the beams of my own eyes in a mirror.
The lives that we must go on with
are also yours. So I go on
down the apartment steps to the hot
streets of July the twenty-second, nineteen
hundred and eighty in Trinidad,
amazed that trees are still green
around the Savannah, over the Queen's
Park benches, amazed that my feet can carry
the stone of the earth, the heavier stone of the head,
and I pass through shade where a curled
blossom falls from a black, forked branch
to the asphalt, soundlessly. No cry.
You knew neither this world nor the next,
and, as for us, whose hearts must never harden
against ourselves, who sit on a park bench
like any calm man in a public garden
watching the bright traffic,
we can only wonder why a seed should envy
our suffering, to flower, to suffer,
to die. Gloria, Perdita, I christen
you in the shade, on the bench,
with no hope of the resurrection.
Pardon. Pardon the pride I have taken
in a woman's agony.

Easter

Anna, my daughter,
you have a black dog
that noses your heel,
selfless as a shadow;
here is a fable
about a black dog:
On the last sunrise
the shadow dressed with Him,
it stretched itself also—
they were two big men
with one job to do.
But life had been lent to one
only for this life.
They strode in silence toward
uncontradicting night.
The rats at the Last Supper
shared crumbs with their shadows,
the shadow of the bread
was shared by the bread;
when the candles lowered,
the shadow felt larger,
so He ordered it to leave;
He said where He was going
it would not be needed,
for there there'd be either
radiance or nothing.
It stopped when He turned

and ordered it home,
then it resumed the scent;
it felt itself stretching
as the sun grew small
like the eyes of the soldiers
receding into holes
under the petrified
serpents on their helmets;
the narrowing pupils
glinted like nailheads,
so before He lay back
it crept between the wood
as if it were the pallet
they had always shared;
it crept between the wood
and the flesh nailed to the wood
and it rose like a black flag
as the crossbeam hoisted
itself and the eyes
closed very slowly
extinguishing the shadow—
everything was nothing.
Then the shadow slunk away,
crawling low on its belly,
and it left there knowing
that never again
would He ever need it;

it reentered the earth,
it didn't eat for three days,
it didn't go out,
then it peeped out carefully
like a mole from its hole,
like a wolf after winter,
like a surreptitious serpent,
looking for those forms
that could give back its shape;
then it ran out when the bells
began making wide rings
and rings of radiance;
it keeps nosing for His shape
and it finds it again, in
the white echo of a pigeon
with its wings extended
like a shirt on a clothesline,
like a white shirt on Monday
dripping from a clothesline,
like the greeting of a scarecrow
or a man yawning
at the end of a field.

Store Bay

I still lug my house on my back—
a mottled, brown shoulder bag
like the turtle's—
to the shadow of a rock,
quivering from sunstroke
and my second divorce.

The sun lives in one place,
his whole year is midsummer,
but a light has gone from the
grass, from the heart's affections.
The far cry of the swimmer
frightens.

In curling surf, two wrestlers
circle the sky's blue vase—
thin ankles, bulging haunch,
silhouettes I once saw
as Hellas. It nearly was.
To the thud of reggaes
from a concrete gazebo,
a yellow glass-bottom launch,
trailing weed from its jaws,
sharks in from the coral gardens
for the next shoal of picnickers.

Two bays around is the sheer
cliff studded with cactus
at Plymouth. Dusk
screeching with cormorants,
wing-flashes like knives,
pelicans scrabbling like fishwives
in the bay's basket.
We went on long drives
in the green evening roads
to buy snapper. After us,
new husbands, new wives.

The sun slits into the metal
horizon; night rocks
like a jukebox.

On fading sand I pass
a mackerel that leapt from its element,
trying to be different—
its eye a golden ring,
married to nothing.
Mistress Mackerel, Mistress Mackerel, I won't be home tonight.
The breakers lance across the blackness once.

The year-long sun
has tired me enough;

I unplug the hotel lamp and lie in bed,
my head full of black surf.
I envy the octopus with ink for blood,
his dangling, disconnected wires
adrift, unmarried.

NORTH

Wales

[FOR NED THOMAS]

Those white flecks cropping the ridges of Snowdon
will thicken their fleece and come wintering down
through the gap between alliterative hills,
through the caesura that let in the Legions,
past the dark disfigured mouths of the chapels,
till a white silence comes to green-throated Wales.
Down rusty gorges, cold rustling gorse,
over rocks hard as consonants, and rain-vowelled shales
sang the shallow-buried ax, helmet, and baldric
before the wet asphalt sibilance of tires.
A plump raven, Plantagenet, unfurls its heraldic
caw over walls that held the cult of the horse.
In blackened cottages with their stony hatred
of industrial fires, a language is shared
like bread to the mouth, white flocks to dark byres.

The Fortunate Traveller

[F O R   S U S A N   S O N T A G]

And I heard a voice in the midst of the four beasts say,
A measure of wheat for a penny,
and three measures of barley for a penny;
and see thou hurt not the oil and the wine.

REVELATION 6 : 6

[I]

It was in winter. Steeples, spires
congealed like holy candles. Rotting snow
flaked from Europe's ceiling. A compact man,
I crossed the canal in a gray overcoat,
on one lapel a crimson buttonhole
for the cold ecstasy of the assassin.
In the square coffin manacled to my wrist:
small countries pleaded through the mesh of graphs,
in treble-spaced, Xeroxed forms to the World Bank
on which I had scrawled the one word, MERCY;

   I sat on a cold bench
under some skeletal lindens.
Two other gentlemen, black skins gone gray
as their identical, belted overcoats,
crossed the white river.
They spoke the stilted French
of their dark river,
whose hooked worm, multiplying its pale sickle,

could thin the harvest of the winter streets.
"Then we can depend on you to get us those tractors?"
"I gave my word."
"May my country ask you why you are doing this, sir?"
Silence.
"You know if you betray us, you cannot hide?"
A tug. Smoke trailing its dark cry.

At the window in Haiti, I remember
a gekko pressed against the hotel glass,
with white palms, concentrating head.
With a child's hands. Mercy, monsieur. Mercy.
Famine sighs like a scythe
across the field of statistics and the desert
is a moving mouth. In the hold of this earth
10,000,000 shoreless souls are drifting.
Somalia: 765,000, their skeletons will go under the tidal sand.
"We'll meet you in Bristol to conclude the agreement?"
Steeples like tribal lances, through congealing fog
the cries of wounded churchbells wrapped in cotton,
gray mist enfolding the conspirator
like a sealed envelope next to its heart.

No one will look up now to see the jet
fade like a weevil through a cloud of flour.
One flies first-class, one is so fortunate.
Like a telescope reversed, the traveller's eye

swiftly screws down the individual sorrow
to an oval nest of antic numerals,
and the iris, interlocking with this globe,
condenses it to zero, then a cloud.
Beetle-black taxi from Heathrow to my flat.
We are roaches,
riddling the state cabinets, entering the dark holes
of power, carapaced in topcoats,
scuttling around columns, signalling for taxis,
with frantic antennae, to other huddles with roaches;
we infect with optimism, and when
the cabinets crack, we are the first
to scuttle, radiating separately
back to Geneva, Bonn, Washington, London.

Under the dripping planes of Hampstead Heath,
I read her letter again, watching the drizzle
disfigure its pleading like mascara. Margo,
I cannot bear to watch the nations cry.
Then the phone: "We will pay you in Bristol."
Days in fetid bedclothes swallowing cold tea,
the phone stifled by the pillow. The telly
a blue storm with soundless snow.
I'd light the gas and see a tiger's tongue.
I was rehearsing the ecstasies of starvation
for what I had to do. *And have not charity.*

I found my pity, desperately researching
the origins of history, from reed-built communes
by sacred lakes, turning with the first sprocketed
water-driven wheels. I smelled imagination
among bestial hides by the gleam of fat,
seeking in all races a common ingenuity.
I envisaged an Africa flooded with such light
as alchemized the first fields of emmer wheat and barley,
when we savages dyed our pale dead with ochre,
and bordered our temples
with the ceremonial vulva of the conch
in the gray epoch of the obsidian adze.
I sowed the Sahara with rippling cereals,
my charity fertilized these aridities.

What was my field? Late sixteenth century.
My field was a dank acre. A Sussex don,
I taught the Jacobean anxieties: *The White Devil*.
Flamineo's torch startles the brooding yews.
The drawn end comes in strides. I loved my Duchess,
the white flame of her soul blown out between
the smoking cypresses. Then I saw children pounce
on green meat with a rat's ferocity.

I called them up and took the train to Bristol,
my blood the Severn's dregs and silver.
On Severn's estuary the pieces flash,

Iscariot's salary, patron saint of spies.
I thought, who cares how many million starve?
Their rising souls will lighten the world's weight
and level its gull-glittering waterline;
we left at sunset down the estuary.

England recedes. The forked white gull
screeches, circling back.
Even the birds are pulled back by their orbit,
even mercy has its magnetic field.
                              Back in the cabin,
I uncap the whisky, the porthole
mists with glaucoma. By the time I'm pissed,
England, England will be
that pale serrated indigo on the sea-line.
"You are so fortunate, you get to see the world—"
Indeed, indeed, sirs, I have seen the world.
Spray splashes the portholes and vision blurs.

Leaning on the hot rail, watching the hot sea,
I saw them far off, kneeling on hot sand
in the pious genuflections of the locust,
as Ponce's armored knees crush Florida
to the funereal fragrance of white lilies.

Now I have come to where the phantoms live,
I have no fear of phantoms, but of the real.
The sabbath benedictions of the islands.
Treble clef of the snail on the scored leaf,
the Tantum Ergo of black choristers
soars through the organ pipes of coconuts.
Across the dirty beach surpliced with lace,
they pass a brown lagoon behind the priest,
pale and unshaven in his frayed soutane,
into the concrete church at Canaries;
as Albert Schweitzer moves to the harmonium
of morning, and to the pluming chimneys,
the groundswell lifts *Lebensraum, Lebensraum.*

Black faces sprinkled with continual dew—
dew on the speckled croton, dew
on the hard leaf of the knotted plum tree,
dew on the elephant ears of the dasheen.
Through Kurtz's teeth, white skull in elephant grass,
the imperial fiction sings. Sunday
wrinkles downriver from the Heart of Darkness.
The heart of darkness is not Africa.
The heart of darkness is the core of fire
in the white center of the holocaust.
The heart of darkness is the rubber claw

selecting a scalpel in antiseptic light,
the hills of children's shoes outside the chimneys,
the tinkling nickel instruments on the white altar;
Jacob, in his last card, sent me these verses:
"Think of a God who doesn't lose His sleep
if trees burst into tears or glaciers weep.
So, aping His indifference, I write now,
not Anno Domini: After Dachau."

[I I I]

The night maid brings a lamp and draws the blinds.
I stay out on the veranda with the stars.
Breakfast congealed to supper on its plate.

There is no sea as restless as my mind.
The promontories snore. They snore like whales.
Cetus, the whale, was Christ.
The ember dies, the sky smokes like an ash heap.
Reeds wash their hands of guilt and the lagoon
is stained. Louder, since it rained,
a gauze of sand flies hisses from the marsh.

Since God is dead, and these are not His stars,
but man-lit, sulphurous, sanctuary lamps,
it's in the heart of darkness of this earth
that backward tribes keep vigil of His Body,
in deya, lampion, and this bedside lamp.
Keep the news from their blissful ignorance.
Like lice, like lice, the hungry of this earth
swarm to the tree of life. If those who starve
like these rain-flies who shed glazed wings in light
grew from sharp shoulder blades their brittle vans
and soared toward that tree, how it would seethe—
ah, Justice! But fires
drench them like vermin, quotas

prevent them, and they remain
compassionate fodder for the travel book,
its paragraphs like windows from a train,
for everywhere that earth shows its rib cage
and the moon goggles with the eyes of children,
we turn away to read. Rimbaud learned that.
                                 Rimbaud, at dusk,
idling his wrist in water past temples
the plumed dates still protect in Roman file,
knew that we cared less for one human face
than for the scrolls in Alexandria's ashes,
that the bright water could not dye his hand
any more than poetry. The dhow's silhouette
moved through the blinding coinage of the river
that, endlessly, until we pay one debt,
shrouds, every night, an ordinary secret.

[I V]

The drawn sword comes in strides.
It stretches for the length of the empty beach;
the fishermen's huts shut their eyes tight.
A frisson shakes the palm trees,
and sweats on the traveller's tree.
They've found out my sanctuary. Philippe, last night:
"It had two gentlemen in the village yesterday, sir,
asking for you while you was in town.
I tell them you was in town. They send to tell you,
there is no hurry. They will be coming back."

In loaves of cloud, *and have not charity*,
the weevil will make a sahara of Kansas,
the ant shall eat Russia.
Their soft teeth shall make, *and have not charity*,
the harvest's desolation,
and the brown globe crack like a begging bowl,
and though you fire oceans of surplus grain,
and have not charity,

still, through thin stalks,
the smoking stubble, stalks
grasshopper: third horseman,
the leather-helmed locust.

The Season of Phantasmal Peace

Then all the nations of birds lifted together
the huge net of the shadows of this earth
in multitudinous dialects, twittering tongues,
stitching and crossing it. They lifted up
the shadows of long pines down trackless slopes,
the shadows of glass-faced towers down evening streets,
the shadow of a frail plant on a city sill—
the net rising soundless as night, the birds' cries soundless, until
there was no longer dusk, or season, decline, or weather,
only this passage of phantasmal light
that not the narrowest shadow dared to sever.

And men could not see, looking up, what the wild geese drew,
what the ospreys trailed behind them in silvery ropes
that flashed in the icy sunlight; they could not hear
battalions of starlings waging peaceful cries,
bearing the net higher, covering this world
like the vines of an orchard, or a mother drawing
the trembling gauze over the trembling eyes
of a child fluttering to sleep;
                              it was the light
that you will see at evening on the side of a hill
in yellow October, and no one hearing knew
what change had brought into the raven's cawing,
the killdeer's screech, the ember-circling chough
such an immense, soundless, and high concern
for the fields and cities where the birds belong,

except it was their seasonal passing, Love,
made seasonless, or, from the high privilege of their birth,
something brighter than pity for the wingless ones
below them who shared dark holes in windows and in houses,
and higher they lifted the net with soundless voices
above all change, betrayals of falling suns,
and this season lasted one moment, like the pause
between dusk and darkness, between fury and peace,
but, for such as our earth is now, it lasted long.